SUCCESSFUL TELEPHONE TECHNIQUES

SUCCESSFUL TELEPHONE TECHNIQUES

How to Improve Your Organisation's Image

Judith Taylor

KOGAN PAGE

First published in 1994

Kogan Page Limited
120 Pentonville Road
London N1 9JN

British Library Cataloguing in Publication Data

A CIP record for this book is available from the British Library.

ISBN 0-7494-1178-3

Typeset by BookEns Ltd, Baldock, Herts.
Printed and bound in Great Britain by Clays Ltd, St Ives plc.

Acknowledgements

The author would like to thank the following for their help: BT Business Publications; Josephine Crane, PR Officer, Mercury Communications Limited; John, Sue, Stella and Jennifer for providing case studies.

Contents

Introduction

Most homes have one. Every office does. Managers who spend a substantial part of their time away from the office tend to carry one around with them. They are to be found on street corners, in railway stations, in shops, restaurants, factories, schools, theatres, pubs, clubs — the telephone is ubiquitous.

Why do we make so much use of the telephone? Most people would answer that it saves time. It is generally quicker to ring someone up than to meet them face to face. If it is quicker it is also likely to be cheaper. You can make personal contact and get instant feedback, that is you can telephone someone with an enquiry and get an answer straight away. Many important business deals are conducted on the telephone.

However, it can be intrusive. 'Cold calls' to private numbers have to be handled sensitively to avoid causing annoyance. You can control the calls you make but not the ones made to you. Many managers would state the telephone as one of their major time-wasters.

Like using a photocopier or a tape recorder, using the telephone requires technical skill. However, unlike other pieces of office equipment, interpersonal skills are also called for; it is these skills, so often neglected, which are the focus of this book.

CHAPTER 1
The Importance of the Telephone

Telephones have been around since 1877 but it's fair to say that many of us still have a love – hate relationship with them. They seem to highlight and exaggerate any inadequacies we have in communicating with other people. You can't make up for a lack of the right word by your facial expression. You may wonder whether the other person is really listening. Sometimes your mind goes blank so that you forget what you had to say, and have to ring back a few minutes later: 'By the way, I forgot to ask you ....' Ending telephone conversations politely but firmly is a problem for many people.

Four good reasons why we use the telephone

With all these difficulties, why do we make so much use of the telephone?

1. The first reason has to be **speed**. It is much quicker to pick up a receiver and dial a number than it is to dictate, write, or type a letter. The problem of finding that the number

you want is busy, or not answering, can be eased, if not altogether solved, by the use of various time-saving facilities such as memories, last number redial, and answering machines.

2. The second reason is **cost**. This may seem surprising at first when you look at the cost of telephone rental and calls. But, in business, you also need to take into account the cost and value to your company of your time and that of any staff working for you. Think also of the time saved which might give you just the edge you need over your competitors. When you take these factors into account the telephone is a very cost-effective means of communication.

3. **Personal contact** is the third reason. There is no visual contact. However, you can hear a voice and build up a mental picture of the person to whom you are speaking. Even without visual contact it is possible to learn a lot about how someone thinks, feels and behaves – and they can learn about you.

4. This leads on to the fourth reason, which is **feedback**. Unlike written communication, feedback via the telephone can be instant, and it is feedback which turns a statement, or a question, into communication.

Communication is concerned, not only with sending a message to another person, but doing what you can to ensure that that message is understood. Feedback tells you that this has happened. It is much easier to get feedback from personal contact with the other person. You can question, explain, criticise, agree, disagree, enlarge, check understanding, express feelings as well as opinions, while the topic is hot. You can do all these things by letter (or more likely letters) but the inevitable delay presents an obstacle.

There are, of course, some occasions when it is better not to use the telephone, for example:

● It is usually easier to talk through really difficult problems face to face as you can judge the other person's reactions and feelings better

- It may be better to write to busy senior people
- If a considered response is required
- Bad news to someone you don't know very well may be better conveyed by letter. Bad news to someone you do know well is best given face to face
- If the information you wish to give is highly confidential
- If a formal record is required
- Complex information is usually clearer when it is set out in writing
- You may wish to avoid discussion with someone
- Cost may be a factor with lengthy long-distance calls. If speed is not essential, it may be better to write
- Writing a brief reply on the bottom of an internal memo takes less time than making several attempts to contact a busy colleague
- As electronic mail becomes more widely used it may replace telephone use when a simple answer or piece of information is needed.

The telephone is a vital piece of equipment. Its importance can be demonstrated by thinking of the uses to which it can be put: selling, buying, explaining, information giving and receiving, discussing, negotiating, arranging, confirming, networking — the list is endless, and these are just business calls. Even contracts and agreements may be agreed by telephone and confirmed later in writing.

Costs and how to control them

BT has two call rates which relate to different times of the day and week; cheap rate 6 pm to 8 am Monday to Friday and all weekend from 6 pm Friday to 8 am Monday, and standard rate at all other times. (There are some differences over bank holidays.) Once connected to the switchboard, it is cheaper to hang up and try again than to hold if the extension you want is busy. Modern facilities such as last number redial will save you time.

The rates for international calls also vary according to the day and the time; the telephone company which supplied your system will be able to give you details. Many organisations are now switching to Mercury for long-distance calls, as these are cheaper, but BT has recently altered some of its charges in the face of competition, and there may be further changes.

Private telephone calls are a thorny problem for organisations. Itemised bills now make it possible to check the use of office telephones, and persistent overuse can be identified and stopped.

Case study

John, an architect, is sole proprietor of a design, advice and build company. He believes the telephone to be vital to his success:

'When the telephone stops ringing, I'm out of business.

'It complements face-to-face contacts with clients, subcontractors, suppliers, etc, but it is not a substitute for this. It keeps things warm, but any business deals must be confirmed in writing. In face-to-face communication you rely heavily on facial expression, etc, which is lost on the telephone, but you can cultivate the art of listening so that you can quickly pick up if someone is bored or frustrated – a sign that you are not getting through.

'A drawback is that people tend to use the telephone too freely – they think it gives instant access to you and make unreasonable demands on your time. The most helpful people are those who have briefed themselves before making a call, rather than thinking aloud.'

Case study

Jennifer is research manager of a large public sector organisation.

'The telephone is very important, not least because as a public service industry we have to conform to performance measurements and telephone handling is considered to be an important point of contact between us and the public, and is also taken as an internal quality service performance measurement. It is taken very seriously by the organisation. In terms of our own particular needs we often have to rely on the co-operation of other staff. For example, we might need a quick job done by the printing office and it's very useful to have established a good pleasant telephone working relationship with people so that when you ring them up and you have to ask them to pull the stops out they will do their best for you. If you have rapport with people on the telephone that can work in your favour.

'As a manager it is important that if I get people to ring up on my behalf they are speaking for me so I want to make sure that this is handled in a proper manner, because it's saying something about me – it's equivalent to someone sending out a letter on your behalf; you want to make sure that it is spelt correctly but you don't want to have to check every letter that goes out. It is saying something about you and your management ability so it is important to me that the people ringing the office get an impression of courtesy and helpfulness and efficiency.'

CHAPTER 2
Professionalism on the Telephone

Communication

We communicate in order to understand and be understood; this is therefore a two-way process. Good communication requires patience, skill and commitment. It requires a message to be sent to a recipient, and that message to be received and understood. The way to discover if it has been received and, if so, whether it has been properly understood, is by feedback. In other words, the other person has to say 'Yes', 'I see', 'I understand', or, conversely 'I don't understand', in which case you have to try to make yourself clearer.

Feedback also allows the receiver of the message to comment on it in some way, and a dialogue may ensue. Most of the time we give and receive feedback naturally, without thinking about it, using a range of verbal and non-verbal signs and signals to show that we are participating in the communication process.

However, this is easier in face-to-face communication than it is on the telephone. There is no doubt that the loss of visual contact is a handicap. In face-to-face conversation we learn a great deal above and beyond the words being used: from facial

One way message giving

$$\text{Sender} \xrightarrow{\hspace{3cm}} (Message) \xrightarrow{\hspace{3cm}} \text{Receiver}$$

Two way communication

$$\text{Sender} \xrightarrow{\hspace{3cm}} (Message) \xrightarrow{\hspace{3cm}} \text{Receiver}$$
Sender
(Receiver)

Receiver
(Sender)

$$\xleftarrow{\hspace{2cm}} (Feedback) \xleftarrow{\hspace{2cm}}$$

expression, the way people use their hands, shrug their shoulders, or shuffle their feet. In the USA, Professor A Mehrabian has found that the total impact of a message is:

7 per cent verbal (words only)
38 per cent vocal (tone of voice)
55 per cent non-verbal (gestures, facial expression).

(Mehrabian, A (1971) *Silent Messages*, Wadsworth, Belmont, California)

On the telephone, therefore, impact is potentially lost unless it is made up in other ways. All you have is your voice and it is important to make it sound clear, positive and interested.

Accents are not important but clarity is. Sounding enthusiastic may be difficult at the end of a long day, but it's worth it.

If you smile it will be heard. This may sound far-fetched, but there are both psychological and physiological reasons for the assertion. First of all, your spirits do rise when you smile. It is extremely difficult to continue to feel gloomy with a smile on your face. Second, the small muscles which lift the corners of the mouth also have an effect on the pitch of the voice, raising it a little and making it sound interested.

Practical points to watch out for are:

Inflection	Try not to talk in a monotone. Make your voice rise and fall.
Tone	This will reflect your attitude.
Rate	Don't speak too quickly. Give the caller time to take in what you have to say.
Enunciation	Speak clearly and never with something in your mouth (pipe smokers and pencil chewers please note!). Be particularly careful with names of people, addresses, etc.

Listening skills

Listening skills are vital in any type of oral communication; on the telephone it is particularly important, not only to listen, but to let the other person know that you are doing so. Let's look at this essential skill in more detail.

There is a difference between hearing, which, unless there is a physical problem, is an easy thing to do, and listening, which is much more difficult and requires concentration. It is virtually impossible to concentrate on two things at once, so those who like to play music while they work can only be hearing the music. In order to listen to it they would have to stop working.

There are a number of things which interfere with good listening. They include:

- *External distractions*, such as noise, other people's activities, the heat or cold of the room, the speaker's mannerisms or appearance.
- *Personal distractions*: indigestion, sleepiness, hunger, anxiety, all interfere with your ability to listen.
- *Daydreaming.* Unless you are really concentrating, words can trigger off trains of thought which take you miles away from the subject in hand. This may be the result of external or personal distractions, or poor speaking.
- *Poor speaking.* You must concentrate even harder to get the message from a poor speaker.

- *Selective listening*. It is very easy to stop listening for a while if the subject seems overfamiliar or boring. But it is easy, if you are guilty of this, to miss important facts or misinterpret the message altogether.
- *Not listening*. A lazy listener condemns a subject matter in advance as being uninteresting, or too technical, or something with which he or she disagrees.
- *Interrupting*. People who interrupt frequently assume that they know what the speaker is going to say, and stop listening. Or they may be too concerned with what they themselves want to say.

There are a number of things which you can do to improve your listening skills:

- Recognise distractions and put them aside.
- Remind yourself of the reasons why you are listening. Be psychologically prepared to listen.
- Try to be open-minded about subjects which you think may be controversial, or uninteresting. Find an area of interest.
- Listen for ideas. The good listener focuses on the main ideas rather than peripheral themes and inessential details.
- Take notes.
- Practise active listening.

Active listening

Active listening will help you to listen and the other person to express him or herself. On the telephone you are restricted to your voice, and cannot nod, smile, frown, etc. To compensate for this make a conscious effort to increase the number of times you say 'Yes', 'Mm', 'I see', or even grunt; this indicates to the other person that you are paying attention. Ask questions, and constantly check for understanding. Say things like 'Am I right in thinking that you need more time before you can produce a final report?' 'Are you saying that we should involve personnel in our discussions?' At the end, summarise what you think has been agreed, and allow the other person time to respond: 'Are we agreed that I will brief the chairman and you will write the report?'

Above all, try to remain alert and interested. It is quite easy to tell when you have lost someone's attention, even on the other end of a telephone.

Asking questions

Anyone who has been involved in selection interviews, for example, will know that it is not easy to get the information you need out of each candidate in a short space of time. Asking the right question in the right way at the right time is an important skill, although it is not always recognised as such.

The main types of question are as follows:

Open. These are designed to encourage people to talk and are useful when you want to explore a topic in a general way. They are most useful at the start of a discussion. You are likely to ask 'Tell me about ...', 'What happened when ...?'

Probing. These will help you to tease out more detailed information. For example, 'What happened next?' 'How did you set about trying to mend it?'

Closed. These are used to establish single, specific facts, and tend to elicit one-word answers: 'What time did this happen?' 'Do you have the receipt?'

Reflective. These questions are often used in counselling and problem solving, and can help to diffuse emotionally charged situations. You repeat back what the other person has said: 'You are unhappy about the way we dealt with your problem?' 'You say you felt upset about the move?'

Leading. These are frequently used but not very helpful except in gaining acceptance of your point of view. 'I suppose you checked it out first?' and 'I take it you haven't approached anyone else?' tend to lead to the answer you expect.

Hypothetical. 'What would happen if ...?' can help people to think about new ideas.

Multiple. A string of questions should be avoided as they

21

only serve to confuse both questioner and the person being questioned.

If your job involves eliciting information from people it is worth spending some time thinking about the questions you ask. The most useful pattern is to start with an open question to get the conversation going and to learn about the situation in broad terms, then narrow the topic down with probing and closed questions in order to check the facts.

Assertiveness on the telephone

Particular problem areas are discussed in Chapter 3, but here we will look at the general principles of assertiveness, which you should find helpful when dealing with other people. But, first, use this exercise to help you to think about how you deal with people on the telephone.

How do you behave on the telephone?
Each of the situations listed has three possible responses. Imagine yourself in each situation, and tick the response which is most like you:

(A) A customer telephones, angry because of a delay to the delivery of his order. It is your job to deal with complaints but he insists on speaking to someone 'more senior'. You:

1. Get annoyed.   ☐
2. Apologise profusely because all the managers are out.   ☐
3. Explain that your job is to take down the facts and see if the problem can be resolved before referring it to a manager.   ☐

(B) When you have a difficult call to make, do you:
1. Keep putting it off?   ☐
2. Plan what to say and how to say it, making the call at the first appropriate time?   ☐

---

3. Make the call when you feel in the mood
    without giving it any particular thought? ☐

(C) When people telephone to try to sell you
    something, do you:
1. Tell them to get lost? ☐
2. Allow yourself to be persuaded to meet them? ☐
3. Say politely but firmly that you do not want
    the item? ☐

(D) A colleague who you know well asks if you can
    help out with her workload. This has happened
    before. You say:
1. I'm fed up with this, Jane. It's not my job to
    help you out when you can't cope. ☐
2. Well, I don't know ... oh, all right. ☐
3. No, Jane, I realise that you are busy.
    However, I can't help you this time as I have
    my own work to do. ☐

(E) You need some figures at short notice for a
    meeting. You telephone the finance office and say:
1. I need information about travel costs for the
    board meeting tomorrow. I'd be grateful if
    you could let me have these figures as a
    matter of urgency. ☐
2. I'm awfully sorry to bother you but I
    just wondered − er − could you possibly
    let me have the figures on − um − travel
    costs some time − well, it's not really urgent
    but if you could let me have them by this
    afternoon .... ☐
3. Look, you're going to have to drop every-
    thing and get me these figures now. ☐

(F) The managing director telephones. You:
1. Panic. ☐
2. Think 'I'm as good as he is any day'. ☐
3. Deal with him efficiently and politely. ☐

(G) In the course of conversation someone criticises your boss. You don't agree. You say:
1. Well, I see what you mean. ☐
2. I don't think that's fair. I get on with her very well. ☐
3. You're just stupid and prejudiced. ☐

(H) You have to tell a senior manager that the course he wanted to attend is fully booked. You:
1. Spend five minutes apologising before getting to the point. ☐
2. Announce the news abruptly and anticipate possible criticism by saying 'It's not my fault, they didn't tell me the closing date'. ☐
3. Explain that the present course is full but the organisers hope to repeat it next year. ☐

(I) The telephone rings while you are talking to a visitor. You answer it and:
1. Try to hold two conversations at once. ☐
2. Say 'I'm busy, you'll have to ring back.' ☐
3. Explain that you have a visitor and ask if you can ring back, giving an anticipated time. ☐

Key:
If you ticked A3, B2, C3, D3, E1, F3, G2, H3, I3, you have behaved in an assertive manner. You state your opinion calmly and firmly, while acknowledging the other person's point of view.

If you ticked A1, B3, C1, D1, E3, F2, G3, H2, I2, you tend to behave aggressively. You allow emotions to get in the way of clear communication, and have little regard for others' feelings or points of view.

If you ticked A2, B1, C2, D2, E2, F1, G1, H1, I1, you are unassertive and rather passive. You tend to let other people walk over you and have difficulty getting them to acknowledge your rights and opinions.

Assertiveness is about dealing with people in a way that is open and honest without being either passive or aggressive. It is a communication skill which enables you to state your needs, feelings and opinions clearly and openly and negotiate with others to reach a mutually satisfactory outcome. By communicating assertively you are less likely to misunderstand or be misunderstood. Assertive behaviour allows you to:

- Express disagreement without creating unnecessary conflict
- Make requests and state views in a confident manner
- Co-operate with others in solving problems so that everybody is reasonably satisfied with the outcome
- Cope with criticism
- Deal with awkward people and awkward situations more effectively.

The important thing is not to get your own way at all costs, but to try to reach a mutually satisfactory outcome.

The following points are particularly relevant to telephone communication:

- Know who you want to speak to and what you wish to say before picking up the receiver.
- When answering the telephone, say who you are clearly and in a positive manner.
- Use a steady tone of voice, speaking clearly and not too fast. If your voice tends to crack or become strained when talking to others, practise some techniques to relax your jaw and shoulders.
- Try to avoid unneccessary padding, 'Um', 'Er', 'I wondered whether perhaps it might be possible for you at some stage to ...' (try 'Would you ...?' instead). Keep 'I'm sorry' for the times you really do want to apologise and don't use it to plug gaps in the conversation or as a means of interrupting the other person.
- Assertive people don't feel inadequate if they don't understand something but will ask for clarification.
- Equally, an assertive person will not feel guilty, cover up or

bluster if he or she does not have the answer to a question, but will admit this and offer to try to find out.

The three strategies outlined below will help you to communicate assertively on the telephone:

Broken record

The title comes from the way the needle will stick on a scratch on a long-playing record and play the same short phrase of music over and over again. This approach can be useful in a situation when you are trying to make a point, but the other person seems to be ignoring your request, or your refusal, perhaps by trying to distract you with other issues. Do not allow yourself to be side-tracked, or drawn into an argument, but choose a form of words with which you feel comfortable, and keep on repeating the statement. For example:

'I am not prepared to rewrite the report to take account of your comments, which arrived after my deadline.'

'My report is complete, and I am not prepared to rewrite it.'

'Please understand that I am not prepared to change my report.'

Empathy

Many people are uncomfortable with refusing a request in an assertive way, feeling that it somehow means they are rejecting the person. Using empathy softens the 'no'. It indicates to the other person that his or her request has been heard, and that the person making the refusal is sorry that they cannot comply. This approach is likely to defuse anger, as anger often arises because people feel that they have been ignored. For example: 'I realise that you are anxious for your comments to be included in the report. However, the deadline has passed, the report is now complete and I am not prepared to rewrite it.'

Workable compromise

A compromise is acceptable if it seems likely to work well for each party. The crucial thing to remember when you are practising assertiveness is to retain your self-respect. For example: 'I am not prepared to rewrite my report to include your comments. However, I could arrange for them to be included as a late submission and tabled at the meeting.'

Summary

To ensure effective communication on the telephone:

> Be Clear,
> Concise,
> Courteous,
> and Control the call.

Be *clear*

- Speak clearly
- Avoid jargon
- Make sure you understand and are understood by giving and asking for feedback.

Be *concise*

- Set objectives for each call
- Know who you want to speak to
- Know what you want to say
- Have any information by you as you make your call.

Be *courteous*

- Don't telephone someone if you are angry
- Don't allow your frustration to show in your voice
- Always be polite
- Use personal names when appropriate

- Listen to the other person's tone of voice for hidden meanings
- Smile.

Control the call by practising assertiveness skills.

Case study

Stella is the switchboard supervisor of a large university.

'The job can be quite stressful because many callers are very demanding. It's a very busy switchboard. We take an average of four-and-a-half thousand calls a day, that's about 135 per 15 minutes. We have to spend time on the majority of calls because many people just don't appear to know what they want. They're vague on the name and they're vague on their enquiry – many times they've got the extension number but they don't seem to want to give it, which adds to the frustration. We also get a lot of general enquiries from the public wanting to know about the college and what we do here, admissions enquiries etc, and people don't always answer their telephones so they keep coming back to us. People don't like answerphones, they do like to speak to a person.

'People can be very rude. I feel that it's because on the telephone they don't see you face to face and it's easier to be rude. You just have to do the best you can, stay as polite as you can, and be helpful.

'Tips? Telling the switchboard when new staff join, for a start. It would be helpful if secretaries could tell us if staff are going to be away for a time. This would be particularly helpful in smaller companies. And a lot of people just answer the telephone with "hello". I've noticed it more and more, but people like to know who they've got through to immediately. Asking for the extension number when you know it saves time.'

CHAPTER 3
Dos and Don'ts

Common ways of upsetting your clients

Let's start with the don'ts and 10 common ways to upset your clients on the telephone:

1. Try not to sound abrupt. No matter how busy you are, when you pick up the telephone you are committed to the call, and must give it your full attention.
2. People at work are much less formal these days. However, this does not mean being casual. Your aim should be to sound both professional and friendly.
3. Saying 'Hello' and nothing else when you answer the telephone is unhelpful and can lead to confusion. Consider the following typical conversation:

'Hello.'
'Hello, is that Brooks Limited?'
'That's right.'
'I want the sales department.'
'Yes.'
'Sorry?'

'This is the sales department.'
'I need to speak to Peter Brown.'
'That's me.'
'Well why didn't you say so in the first place?'

Would it not have saved time and frustration to say 'Good morning, Brooks sales department, Peter Brown speaking'?

This is such a common problem that it is worth discussing it in some detail. Help your caller by saying, at the very least 'Good morning/afternoon', and your name. This may be all that is needed if yours is a small organisation or if the call is an internal one or has come through the switchboard, but if external calls come direct to you you will need to give more information. It is best to say 'Good morning/afternoon' first, as this gives the caller time to adjust their hearing to the sound of your voice. It also allows for any slight delay in connecting your call.

4. Try not to delay in answering a call. This may be a problem for busy managers. However, it is a great source of irritation for people if their calls are ignored or only answered after a long delay. Telephones should be answered within three or four rings.

If you have a piece of work you simply must finish, or a visitor you need to spend time with, there are three things you can do:

1. Divert your calls to a secretary or colleague
2. Advise switchboard that you are unable to take any calls
3. Use an answering machine.

(Beware of making yourself too inaccessible, however.)

5. If you are in a hurry to be somewhere else, try not to sound impatient. Say something like, 'I'm afraid I can't give this sufficient attention now as I have a meeting to attend. Could I think it over and call you back tomorrow?' If you use this method, agree a convenient time for calling back – and don't forget to do so!

6. Avoid jargon. The *Shorter Oxford Dictionary* defines jargon as '... the terminology of a science or art, or the cant of a

class, sect, trade, or profession'. It is acceptable to use jargon among members of the same profession, but it should only be used if you are sure it will be understood by the other person. Don't assume this, however, especially when talking to people new to the organisation, or from outside. If in doubt, miss it out.

7. Do not imagine that by placing your hand over the mouthpiece you can prevent the caller from hearing what you are saying. Modern handsets contain a chip which means that the whole shell acts as a pick-up. Your telephone may have a 'hold' or secrecy facility, but it is safest not to say anything you do not wish the other person to hear while you are still connected.

8. Never try to speak with something in your mouth, whether this is a pen, cigarette, finger or sandwich. Not only does it sound rude, but it makes your speech indistinct.

9. Don't be embarrassed by pauses. People need thinking time and there are gaps in any conversation. Even though these gaps are more difficult to accept on the telephone because you cannot see the other person's face, do not feel compelled to fill them with meaningless talk.

10. Don't try to talk to two people at once.

Getting it right

The following are 10 steps to success on the telephone:

Making calls

1. Getting your call in *first* will help you to stay in control.
2. *Plan* your calls. Work out beforehand what you want to say, who you want to say it to, and your objectives — what you hope to achieve by the call. Anticipate further questions and have any relevant information in front of you when you telephone.

3. Ask *clearly* for the person you want and the department. Use the extension number if you know it. (Make a note to include your extension number on correspondence.)

   If secretaries ask for the *purpose* of your call, tell them (unless, of course, it is truly confidential). Secretaries these days are often employed as members of the management team, and may well be the most appropriate people to deal with in the first instance.

4. When you get through, state *clearly* who you are and the reason for your call. Be as clear and concise as possible (remember, most people give the telephone as one of their main time-wasters).

5. If what you have to say is long or confidential, it might be a good idea to *check* with the person you are calling if it is a convenient time to discuss it.

Receiving calls

6. *Smile* when you answer the telephone.

7. The exact form of *greeting* may be determined by policy, the size of your organisation and its relation to the switchboard, etc, but you should always sound lively and interested in what the caller has to say. Don't just say 'Yes' or 'Hello'. Do say 'Good morning' or 'Good afternoon', do identify yourself and/or your department and, if you want to sound really helpful, add 'How may I help you?'

8. Use of *names*. Many companies encourage staff to use their customers' names as much as possible to increase the feeling of intimacy and friendliness. Learn as much as you can about regular customers and show interest in them.

   We would, however, add a word of warning: many people, especially older people, do not like to be addressed by their first name too early in the conversation. Until you know people, it is best to err on the side of formality: 'I'll check that for you, Mr Green', or 'Ms Jones, I'm so pleased you called' sound polite and friendly.

   If you are taking down someone's name and address, ask

yourself if it is really necessary to know whether a woman is married or not. 'Ms' is a convenient term which can be applied to all women.

9. *Ending.* Sometimes people have difficulty finishing a call. Be assertive about it. What you say will be affected by the other person, but consider the following phrases:

'Thank you for your time ... I know how busy you are so I won't keep you any longer ... .'

'It's been nice talking to you, I'll be in touch again next week.'

'I'll write to confirm our agreement; you should get the letter next week.'

'I'll call again when I have had time to think about this.'

'I have appreciated the opportunity to talk to you, Mr Green.'

The use of their names will often distract verbose people from what they are saying to what you are saying. 'White' lies are not normally to be recommended, but if you are really hard pressed you could try, 'Sorry, I'm wanted on the other phone/there's a visitor waiting to see me.'

10. We tend to remember best things we say at the start and the end of conversations, so it is a good plan to repeat back the gist of the conversation, and *summarise* any arrangements made. Use phrases like, 'As I understand it ...', 'I think we agreed that ....' Make it clear how matters are left.

Special areas to consider

Transferring calls

The first tip is get to know your system so that you can transfer calls quickly and efficiently. The second is to remember that being transferred can be very frustrating for the caller, so do keep the person informed about what is going on. Try the following steps:

● Explain to the caller what you are doing.

- Check with the recipient before putting the call through whether or not they can help.
- If there is a delay, return to the caller to explain and ask if they wish to continue holding.
- If there is a real problem, ask if you can have the caller rung back when you have found someone to help.
- When you return to a caller who has been waiting, check whether he or she is still there before transferring.

Messages

Giving messages

- Always allow time for the other person to write the message down, pausing after each phrase.
- When dictating names or numbers, pause after meaningful groups of numbers or letters, for example 071/323/1234 or H—a—z—e—l/t—r—e—e/L—a—n—e/, G—u—i—l—d —f—o—r—d,/ S—u—r—r—e—y.
- Check that the other person has taken the message correctly.

Receiving messages

- *Always* write messages down as soon as you can. Try to keep a separate pad just for messages, rather than scraps of paper and used envelopes. Specially printed message pads are a good idea.
- Do not hesitate to ask for the message to be repeated, or for unfamiliar words to be spelt out.
- Read back the message to check that it is correct.

Dealing with difficult situations

Overall, the best advice is: stay in control of your emotions. Never telephone someone when you are feeling angry. It is also a good tip to make the call, rather than waiting to be called – that way you have a better chance of staying in control. And make difficult calls early in the day, so that worrying about them won't get in the way of everything else you have to do.

Don't forget to listen to the tone of voice for hidden messages – for example, someone saying 'I understand' in a very hesitant way may in fact be saying 'I don't know if I do understand'.

Learn one or two relaxation techniques to help you when you have to make difficult calls which are likely to cause you anxiety. The following are easy to do, wherever you are, and have been found to be very helpful:

- Take two deep breaths, breathing from the diaphragm, and each time let the breath out as slowly as possible, feeling the tension leave your body at the same time as the breath.
- Tense all your muscles, then relax them, and notice the difference. Become aware of any build-up of tension in your body. Be particularly aware of your jaw and shoulders, as tension here can affect your voice.

The other person may also be experiencing anxiety. Your organisation may be very familiar to you but can seem large and frightening to someone calling from outside (and tension can make nervousness sound like aggression in some people). If you are friendly and helpful and patient, you will encourage the other person to relax and say what they have to say more clearly.

The following points will help you to deal with a particular situation:

Making a complaint

- Before you make the call, decide on your objectives. What do you hope to get out of making the complaint? A hearing, an apology, a settlement? What are you prepared to settle for?
- Marshal your facts and decide on a strategy. Be careful in your choice of words.

- Practise the broken record technique (see Chapter 2).

Receiving complaints

- Stop whatever you are doing and give the caller your full attention. Let him or her feel that they are being taken seriously.
- Listen to what is being said, concentrating on the facts rather than the emotions, and write these down.
- Allow the caller to have his or her say. Don't interrupt too soon.
- Show empathy (see Chapter 2) and apologise for any mistake which may have been made. Try to avoid apologising for something which is not your fault, and equally avoid putting the blame on someone else, the system, or the complainer. Don't agree with wild statements but say something like, 'I can understand why you feel that way'.
- Don't make rash promises and keep any promises you do make. Deal with the matter quickly.
- Keep the complainer informed of progress if this seems to be slow.
- If the complaint was justified, avoid making the same mistake again.

Aggression

- Keep calm and try not to be drawn into an emotional state yourself, as this will only escalate the problem. Listen to the facts.
- Don't interrupt too soon but allow the person to let off steam.
- Recognise the person's anger and show understanding of its cause, but don't be drawn into making promises which cannot be kept, or ultimately unhelpful alternative suggestions.
- If the answer is no, say so and keep on saying so, calmly and reasonably. Try not to be drawn into an argument.

Requests for confidential information

- Confidential information should never be given out over the telephone as you have no proof of the caller's identity.
- The normal procedure would be to ask for the request to be made in writing. If the matter is urgent (for example, the police) ask if you or the individual concerned can phone back.
- The 1984 Data Protection Act adds legal backing to the rule that personal data should only be released when properly authorised. Check further details with your Data Protection Officer.
- Learn to say no, politely but firmly.

Case study

Jennifer: 'We get calls from the media who can be very insistent. I tell my staff to be courteous and helpful, but not to give any information away. They may want to speak to me personally in which case I ask my clerk to take a message. We don't fob them off by saying I will speak to them if I have no intention of doing so. Instead I would say something like, 'I think it would be more helpful if you talked to our press office'. As I am out a lot my clerk has to make judgements about this sort of thing but I don't want her to be subject to people's irritation, so if she feels something is getting too difficult for her to handle I ask her to take a message and then I will get on to it.

'I try not to ask her to lie for me but occasionally I will ask her to say that I am unavailable if I am feeling particularly harassed.

'When I have to deal with difficult calls I try to prepare, but I don't over-rehearse because you can be thrown if the other person says something unexpected. I start by asking, "How can I help?" or "I understand you have a problem, perhaps we can

---

discuss this". A pleasant opening sometimes diffuses any anger. I make the assumption that most people given a chance would like to deal with problems in a civilised way.

If it is a really difficult problem, I usually suggest that it might be better either to write in or to arrange a face-to-face meeting. You have to try to judge how the other person is responding, and you only have his or her tone of voice to go by. If they are in an emotional state I will usually suggest that I call back when the person has had time to calm down.

'I always follow up a difficult telephone conversation with a note summarising any agreement we reached.

'If you think someone wants to have a row with you it can give you a slight edge if you get your call in first. The most difficult calls are when we have made a mistake. I try not to put them off for too long. If I try to ignore them they keep niggling away at me.'

Effective use of the switchboard

Often there is conflict between switchboard operators and other staff. Much of this can be avoided if both parties are prepared to see things from the other person's point of view!

Tips for switchboard operators

1. Answer the call as quickly as possible – after three rings is ideal.
2. Answer the call in a clear, friendly voice. Don't say the name of your organisation too quickly, and do finish what you are saying before transferring the call – all too often one hears 'I'm just putting you through to ...' and the rest is lost.

3. Announce the call clearly, and give the recipient time to respond before putting it through.
4. If the line is busy, you need to ask the caller whether they want to hold or call back. Placing calls on hold and retrieving them is a skilled business; the crucial things to remember are *do* tell callers what you are doing, and *don't* leave them holding for too long without checking back.
5. You should only intrude on a call if it is really necessary; if it is, try to be brief and polite.
6. Your organisation may have different methods of dealing with external and internal calls, but in any event every call needs to be dealt with courteously and efficiently.

Checklist for managers

- Is your switchboard kept up to date with changes of name, extensions, etc? Most operators will need not only an alphabetical list, but also a list of who is responsible for what within departments, or other areas of activity.
- Are your switchboard operators provided with training in the products or services provided by your organisation?
- Are staff familiar with how the switchboard works, and who the operators are? Are secretaries trained to operate it when the operator is not available?
- Is it clear which numbers can be dialled direct and which must go through the operator?
- If the operator has to get a call for you, who is responsible for looking up the number?
- If you ask the operator to get you a call, do you tell him or her if you are called away from your desk?
- Do you tell the switchboard if your office or work area is going to be unattended? (This may not be feasible in large organisations.)
- Are there any rules about leaving messages at the switchboard?

Using answering machines

Answering machines are now so common that there can be very few people who have not encountered one. This does not mean, however, that they are universally popular. Here are some suggestions for making effective use of answering machines:

- Leave a friendly, non-threatening message on your own machine. (A well-known management consultant starts her message by saying, 'This is so and so and a friendly answering machine'.) Say who you are, apologise for not being available, and encourage the caller to leave a brief message: 'Please leave your name and telephone number and we will call you back as soon as possible'; if there is a time limit on messages, say so. It is also a good idea to ask people to give the date and time of their call.
- Don't forget to phone back.

If you encounter someone else's machine, don't panic. The outgoing message gives you time to clear your thoughts. Don't attempt to give a long message – your name, number, date and time of call, and a brief account of the reason for the call is sufficient. Say goodbye if you would otherwise feel uncomfortable, but it is not necessary. Treat the answering machine as a verbal message pad.

Case study

Here's **John** again:

'An answering machine is esssential because of working alone. It acts as a buffer between me and the outside world when I don't want to be interrupted, but the only way it can work is if I respond rapidly to any calls which are left so that people know if they leave a message they will get an answer and are not just being fobbed off.

'On my first contact I tell people I have a machine and encourage them to use it. Once they have got used to the idea they are quite happy to use it. The main problems are people who waffle, and others who put the receiver down without leaving a message — the calls are logged but I can't find them, which is a waste of time.

'I'm thinking now of getting a business system which combines answering machine, fax machine and telephone. Telecommunications are moving forward and in time I'll be able to order materials and interface directly with banks, etc.'

CHAPTER 4

Training your Staff

All managers have a responsibility for the training and development of their staff. Even managers who work in large organisations, with well-resourced training units, should be prepared to monitor training needs and discuss with members of staff the purposes of any training which might be organised for them.

It is important to use the telephone courteously and effectively yourself; it is no good instilling good practice into your sales team if you continue to snatch up the receiver and bark 'Hello!' into it yourself.

It is also worth remembering that junior staff, especially clerical staff, may be the first point of contact after the switchboard for other staff or members of the public. They may have to deal with all sorts of problems and must decide whether to try to handle these themselves, or hand them on to someone else.

First impressions are important, and do last. We have all encountered someone for the first time who sounded bad-tempered, or curt. However much that person improves on acquaintance, it is hard to forget all about that first encounter. The memory stays. And if the person doesn't get the chance to improve – if you never speak to him or her again – you will remember that bad-tempered person who upset you one morning. As the saying goes: 'You never get a second chance to make a first impression.'

Training courses for secretaries and other clerical staff are generally set up not only to improve telephone techniques but also to develop confidence. Sales staff will need all this and, in addition, training in cold-calling, negotiating, closing sales, etc.

It is important for all staff to be familiar with the telephone system and its facilities so that they are confident and comfortable while using it. Give new staff the opportunity to visit the switchboard and meet the operators (and, incidentally, make sure that the switchboard knows the names of new staff). Training may be carried out by the system provider, outside consultants or internal training staff.

Junior staff

Junior staff will also need training activities designed to boost confidence and enhance interpersonal skills. Special equipment is available which enables both sides of a real or mock call to be heard by the trainer via a loudspeaker, or else by recording. The handling of the call can then be analysed and discussed. Most trainers will devise some calls or case studies which suit your organisation and use these for training purposes. The trainer usually acts the part of the 'difficult customer', for example, and the trainee should be him or herself as far as possible.

A suggested course programme for newly appointed clerical and secretarial staff is given below, together with some possible case studies:

Day 1

Morning	Induction into the organisation. People, products, services. Where to find information.
14.30	Visit to the switchboard.
15.15	Tea.
15.30	Using the organisation's telephone system.
17.00	End.

Day 2

09.00	Introductions.
09.30	Particular problems. Small groups discuss particular likes and dislikes about making and receiving telephone calls, which are then written up on flip chart paper and pinned around the room. It is often helpful to break these down into People and Technical problems. They form an agenda for the rest of the day.
10.00	One-sided communication. Participants are divided into pairs and are asked to seat themselves back to back. One person in each pair is given a diagram to describe to the other person. The diagram should be two-dimensional but reasonably complex, for example interlocking geometric shapes. The listener has to copy this down but is not allowed to speak. Pairs then compare notes. The exercise may be repeated with a different diagram, but this time the listener is allowed to ask questions. These exercises form the basis for discussion about giving explanations, the importance of feedback, etc.
10.30	Coffee.
10.45	Skills when dealing with people. General and listening skills. Questioning techniques. Good practice.
11.45	Dealing with difficult situations: • Complaints • Aggression • Cultural differences.
12.45	Lunch.
14.00	Introduction to practical exercises.
14.15	Practical exercise using case studies and special telephone equipment, trainers giving feedback. If this approach is used, there should be no more

than three or four trainees per trainer. The exercise may be carried out without equipment by dividing trainees into threes, two people sitting back to back 'acting' the roles, the third member observing and commenting. Roles are changed to allow everyone to take part. The trainers must circulate around the groups.

16.00	Tea.
16.15	Refer to problems identified at start of day and deal with any not covered.
16.45	Summary and round up. Action plans.
17.15	End.

Case study 1

Receiver

Two weeks ago you opened a memo from the marketing manager, asking your boss, John Weekes, to provide some sales statistics for a meeting. You placed this on top of the mail when you took it in, but then forgot about it. The marketing manager telephones the day of the meeting and asks for the figures. Your boss is out and you know there is no way you can get the information to him in time for the meeting. How do you handle this?

Caller

You are particularly annoyed because you have only just remembered the statistics yourself. You also remember previous occasions when you have had to remind John Weekes about things which he should have remembered for himself. Though not absolutely essential for the meeting, the information would have provided a useful basis for discussion.

Case study 2

Receiver
You work in a busy general office and frequently have to deal with telephone calls which have nothing to do with your work. Switchboard, in particular, tend to direct any calls which they are unsure about to you. You are getting rather tired of this.

One day you receive a call from someone wanting further details of a public lecture which has been advertised in the press. She is rather vague about it. You do not have the details, nor do you know who does.

Caller
You have read in the paper about a public lecture to be held at your local university on 'Victorians and Literature'. You want to know whether it is necessary to book tickets in advance. You have already been through three departments – Information, Academic and Admissions. You are beginning to wish you had never started this enquiry, but you are keen to go to the lecture. What do you say?

Case study 3

Receiver
You are alone in the office when someone telephones to say that her mother has just died and she therefore wishes to cancel her mother's order for new curtains and have her 50 per cent deposit refunded. You know that the material has been ordered and sent to the makers. Your company's policy is that deposits are nonrefundable. What do you say?

Caller
Your mother has just died and you are very upset. You are anxious to clear up her outstanding affairs as quickly as possible. You know that she was a long-standing customer.

Case study 4

Receiver
You work for the local electricity board. A new customer telephones, very angry, because he has been sent a final reminder to pay his bill even though he opted to pay by direct debit.

Caller
You recently moved house and are getting very irritated with all the things which seem to be going wrong. Every service which you have used has been inefficient and incompetent. The final straw is a 'red' reminder from the electricity board, despite the fact that you completed the form opting for direct debit. You consider that you have been very patient so far, but this time you decide to tell the person who answers the phone exactly what you think.

Sales staff

Sales staff will need additional training to help them deal with incoming and outgoing calls. Outgoing calls will include calls to existing customers, and 'cold calls'. Areas which should be covered include:

- Gaining confidence
- Planning and structuring a sales call
- Effective presentation of the product or service
- Listening, questioning and speaking

- The art of friendly persuasion
- Closing the sale
- Follow-up calls.

Case study

Sue works for a partner in a large firm of solicitors. 'I take all my boss's calls from different clients if he's out of the office. If the matter is urgent I try to find out what it relates to and possibly find someone else who can help, especially if my boss isn't going to be available for several hours. I think it's better to take his or her name and phone number, find out what it's about, and say I'll try to get someone to phone back, rather than keep them hanging on.

'Apart from that I communicate with secretaries in different departments, arrange meetings, etc. Being a partner he often entertains clients and I have to use the phone to organise dates, rooms, lunches, etc.

'Yes, people can be difficult sometimes. The best thing is to stay calm and try to be diplomatic. I think the most important thing is always be polite, even if the person gets a bit agitated, even rude on occasions. As long as you can stay polite, it usually saves the day in the end, and of course do your best to get someone to help them as soon as possible.

'When making calls it's a good idea to look through the file to start with to find out who you need to speak to, so that you can answer if you are asked questions. When receiving calls the most irritating thing is when I ask the other person for his or her telephone number so that I can write it on the message and so many people will say "He's got it", or "You know it"; dealing with so many clients we can't possibly remember everyone, and it's a waste of my time to have to go to the file and look it up.'

CHAPTER 5
Technical Matters

At the present time there are two national telephone networks, one operated by British Telecom (BT) and the other by Mercury. Other companies have applied for licences to run national or local networks, and the picture may be very different in a few years' time. BT and Mercury are in competition to provide better quality, more flexible services to business and private customers. There are now fewer differences between them as BT offers itemised bills and cheaper long-distance calls.

If you want to use Mercury's services you need to buy a Mercury-compatible phone with a button marked Mercury or M, which will also have an application form for a Mercury Personal Identification Number (PIN). This must be programmed into the Mercury button on the telephone and the button pressed to switch long-distance or international calls to the Mercury network. The Mercury service is also available through some local cable television operators. A new initiative is 'Residential 132' which enables you to use the service without a PIN code via your local exchange by dialling 132 before making long-distance calls.

Technological innovations are rapidly increasing, and for up-to-the-minute information about which system is best for you, visit a shop specialising in telecommunications or contact one of the companies direct. A list of contacts and addresses is given at the end of the book. BT also produces a number of useful publications and catalogues.

In this chapter we will restrict ourselves to some of the most popular and readily available technical features.

Features of telephone systems and services available

Types of telephone

Tone phones, which produce electronic bleeps or tones as opposed to the electrical clicks or pulses produced by pulse phones, are quicker and more versatile. However, some types of local telephone exchange do not accept tone dialling. For this reason, nearly all new telephones can be switched between tone and pulse.

Features available on most modern phones include:

- *Hands free* – calls can be made and conversations held without lifting the receiver, using a built-in microphone and loudspeaker.
- *Last number redial* – the last number dialled is held in the memory and can be automatically redialled by pressing a button.
- *Ringer volume control* – the volume of ringing can be adjusted.
- *Speech volume control* – the volume of your or your caller's voice can be adjusted.
- *Mute or secrecy button* – this allows you to speak to someone else in the room without your caller hearing the conversation.
- *Memory* – telephone numbers can be stored in the memory and dialled automatically by pressing one or two buttons.

Network services

Network services require connection to a digital exchange via a single line and a tone dialling telephone. Facilities include:

- *Call waiting* – callers hear a message asking them to hold on if your line is busy. At the same time you hear a bleep to let you know that someone else is on the line. You then have a choice of finishing your original conversation quickly, or putting that caller on hold while you deal with the second call.
- *Call diversion* – this enables you to divert calls from the phone you work from to any other, even a mobile, simply by pressing a few buttons.
- *Three-way calling* – this enables three people to talk together at the same time.
- *Charge advice* – by keying in a simple code before you make a call you can find out exactly how much it has cost. After you hang up your phone rings and an electronic 'voice' reports the length of your call and the cost.
- *Reminder call* – if you key in a code and the time you want to be woken or reminded, the phone will ring at that time.

Answering machines

The use of answering machines has been discussed in Chapter 2. There are many different models on the market. Some include a handset and can be used as a normal telephone. Otherwise you may need a telephone socket doubler to connect alongside your telephone. Some answering machines have remote controllers, so that you can listen to your messages from a distance – even abroad.

Mobile telephones

Mobile phones are more correctly known as cellular phones. They operate via a network of radio transmitters and receiver masts; the area covered by each mast is called a cell, which interlocks with other cells across the country. All you need to make and receive calls is an aerial and the handset or receiver. You will also need to subscribe to one of the cellular networks to enable you to use the service. Further information is available from BT or Mercury, both cellnet service providers, or from a telephone shop.

Mobile phones are extremely useful for people on the move. As it is now illegal to hold a telephone to make a call while driving, make sure that the model you choose has an in-car kit which enables it to be powered via the car battery.

The use of mobile phones will change over the next few years. Analogue systems will be replaced by digital ones, which will be clearer and more reliable, and should be available across Europe. Personal Communications Networks (PCNs) are a new form of telephone system based on radio. All PCN calls will be transmitted digitally, and will be cheaper to use. Phone numbers will be personal, and will not change when a customer moves to a new home, or buys a new phone.

Paging

Pagers are small radio receivers which receive messages via radio waves. Several companies, including BT, Mercury and Racal, offer nationwide services, and there are many regional services.

Voice messaging systems

These resemble networks of answering machines operated directly by Mercury, BT and the mobile service operators. Recorded messages can be sent from, and received through, a subscriber's own 'central mailbox'. Dialling a code number from any tone telephone opens the mailbox and messages can be stored, retrieved, deleted and redirected to and from other mailboxes on the system.

Teleconferencing

Teleconferencing enables you to hold meetings and conferences by phone, video link or tv over virtually any distance. The options are:

Audio-conferencing. BT's Conference Call bureau can link between 3 and 60 locations, nationally and internationally, between 07.30 and 22.00 Mondays to Fridays or 08.30 to 22.00 Saturdays and Sundays. BT can dial out to each person taking part to set up the conference call, or you can dial in to join the call. You don't need any special equipment other than a normal telephone, although BT offers a range of loudspeaking terminals if groups of people at different locations want to take an active part in the meeting.

Video-conferencing. People at two or more locations can be brought together to take part in meetings or conferences, either through BT's public video-conferencing centres, or by installing your own equipment on your premises. This enables meetings to be held as if everyone were in the same room. You can use slides or videos, and show close-ups of pictures, documents or objects.

Marketing services

BT can offer a number of services to help businesses:

- *0800* – anyone can phone you at no cost to themselves when you give them a BT 0800 number to use. There is also an international 0800 service available.
- *0345* – this allows your customers to call you from anywhere in the UK for the cost of a local call. You pay the remaining charge.
- *FreeFone name* – the caller dials the operator and asks for your company's personal identifying FreeFone name, enabling them to telephone you free of charge.
- *Call forwarding* – customers are provided with a local number to ring any time. Calls are automatically intercepted

at the local exchange and redirected to wherever your telephones are being operated.

Payphones

BT and Mercury are the only companies which supply public payphones nationwide. Each company has its own phonecards, and many payphones now take credit cards as well. Some BT payphones take cash. Payphones are now available on intercity trains. BT also offers a chargecard, which enables you to make calls from virtually any phone in the UK and charge it to your own business or home phone bill. This service is free — you pay only for the cost of the calls you make.

Videophones

Videophones are now on the market; the current price of BT's Relate 2000 is £399 for one and £749 for a pair (April 1994). A videophone looks very like a normal telephone, and has all the regular facilities such as last number redial, but with a colour, fold-down screen attached. It has a self-viewing facility, so that you can check your appearance before answering, and you can choose whether you want to be seen, by raising the screen and pressing a button. BT videophone call charges are exactly the same as using a normal telephone.

Teleworking

Both Mercury and BT are concerned to give as much support as possible to people working from home, either running their own businesses, or as employees of a company. The development of the telephone facilities described above, linked to fax machines, personal computers and modems, have made it possible for many people to work largely from home, and it has been estimated by BT that 2.5 million people will be teleworking by 1995.

The future

In future, all telephone networks will be completely digital. Telephone exchanges will be able to handle all forms of information — speech, text, computer data, and still and moving pictures. This is called an Integrated Service Digital Network (ISDN). Not only will transmission be clearer and faster, but many additional services will be available via the telephone. You will be able temporarily to redivert your calls when on holiday, order products, goods or services, and have access to a wide range of information services.

Contacts

British Approvals Board for Telecommunications (BABT): The Board responsible for setting the standards for and regulating telecommunications equipment.   **0932 222289**

BT   **FreeFone 0800 800 876**

Mercury Communications   **FreeCall 0500 500 194**

Mercury One-2-One PCN
Service   **FreeCall 0500 500 121**

Office of Telecommunications (Oftel): A non-ministerial government department which oversees and regulates the telecommunications industry. It can supply a list of British Standard approved installers and maintainers of equipment.
071-634 8700

Telecom Users Association (TUA): The organisation representing small and medium-sized businesses and domestic users of telephone services.   **081-445 0996**

Telecommunications Industry Association (TIA): The TIA, which operates its own quality code and encourages British Standards approval, represents most of the better equipment dealers, installers and maintainers, and will supply a list of those in your area.   **071-351 7115**

Glossary

Abbreviated dialling

Regularly called numbers can be given short codes for faster dialling.

BABT

The British Approvals Board for Telecommunications grants the 'green spot' found on all equipment which may legally be connected to any public telecommunications network.

Cellular

The technology behind mobile and car phones, using radio transmitters/receivers covering one area or cell. Cells are linked together to provide service across most of the country.

Cordless

Low-frequency radio technology used for on-site cordless phones.

CT2

Cordless technology which enables calls to be made from public call points using a portable handset.

DTMF

Dial Tone Multi Frequency – the type of 'beep' generated by your phone on dialling which enables access to services such as DDI (Direct Dialling In) or telephone shopping services.

Inductive coupler

Device to help hearing-aid wearers hear more clearly if they switch their aid to the 'T' position.

ISDN

International digital network of the future, offering powerful, flexible transmission of all types of information via telephone networks.

LCR

Least Cost Routing. A software mechanism which enables calls to be sent automatically via the cheapest route.

LD

Loop disconnect. A type of pulse code dial signalling between the telephone and local exchange.

Modem

A device which sits between computer and telephone converting computer data to a format suitable for transmission over the public telephone network.

PABX

Private Automatic Branch Exchange – a switchboard.

PIN

Personal Identification Number.

PSTN

Public Switched Telephone Network – refers to both the BT and Mercury national networks.

Pulse

A form of dialling signal, generally used with analogue systems.

Remote access   Enables you to pick up answering machine access messages while you are away from the telephone.

REN   Ringing Equivalent Number. The number on the bottom of your phone, fax or answerphone which denotes how many items may be used on a single line. A single line supports pieces of equipment with a total REN of 4.

Tone   Electronic dialling signal.

Useful Books to Read

Ken and Kate Back (1982) *Assertiveness at Work*, McGraw-Hill.
Bert Decker (1988) *How to Communicate Effectively*, Kogan Page.
Peter Honey (1986) *Telephone Behaviour: The Power and the Perils*, Video Arts.
Ian MacKay (1990) *A Guide to Asking Questions*, British Association for Commercial and Industrial Education (BACIE).
Ian MacKay (1990) *A Guide to Listening*, BACIE.
Jane Madders (1979) *Stress and Relaxation*, Martin Dunitz.
Various booklets published by BT Business Publications (telephone 0800 800876).